Life tł Poetry

Aleida Tavares

MAPLE
PUBLISHERS

Life Through Poetry

Author: Aleida Tavares

Copyright © Aleida Tavares (2023)

The right of Aleida Tavares to be identified as author of this work has been asserted by the author in accordance with section 77 and 78 of the Copyright, Designs and Patents Act 1988.

First Published in 2023

ISBN 978-1-83538-007-9 (Paperback)
          978-1-83538-008-6 (E-Book)

Cover Design and Book Layout by:
    White Magic Studios
    www.whitemagicstudios.co.uk

Published by:
    Maple Publishers
    Fairbourne Drive, Atterbury,
    Milton Keynes,
    MK10 9RG, UK
    www.maplepublishers.com

CONTENTS

Something about you

Some days, I wake up thinking about you,
About a lot of things that happened to us
That I can't alter,
Because the outcome is the outcome
No matter how often I go over them.

If it didn't happen, it was for a reason,
That is what I need to focus on.

But,

Last night, I had a vision.

Vision of you playing cards with my family,
Vision of us all, bonding together,
Vision of us two playing
Partners, in game and life too;
It was real, it was fun.

We played against two,
In my aunt's room,
So attuned, so silent
They stared curious.

A solid, but only a
Dream, that is what it was,

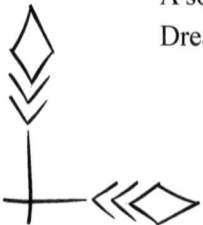

Even though,
It seemed so real.
Down on the bus I was,
Ruffling through my phone,
When I came upon your picture.

I smiled instantly, I beamed actually;
Some eyes were on me, but I couldn't care,
I was too busy staring,

I love how happy you are in it,
I love how true to you it is,
Those unmissable duchenne marks
That I –

I love you,
That is the truth;
No matter how hard I have tried not to sometimes,
Right now, that is the truth.

You

Today I wanted to message you, and
Wish you a good day, I don't know why.

I don't know if it was because,
The weather was nice and dry, or
Because my friend needed a shoulder to cry.

I don't know why,
I just know that
I wanted to wish you a good day,
But I didn't.

I didn't because I felt scared and unsure.
Unsure how you would receive it.
Unsure if would want it, because
It has been a while.

A while since things stopped making sense to me,
A while since I felt angry,
A while,
Still, I wanted you to have a good day,
Every day.

I don't know why you bug me so much,
After all these years,
I don't know why.

I only know that I dwelled on it the entire morning.
On the train, on the tube,
Even at school, where I am meant to forget about you, but
Rarely do.

It has been a long time since we sat and talked,
Since I looked you in the eyes,
Since I had you in front of me.

It has been a long time and
I miss that, I miss them,
I miss how I used to study them
While you talked to me.

For too long,
I wanted to tell you that
They were the first thing that drew me to you, that
They were the portal, my portal.

I still remember how I felt
The first time I paid attention to them,
Their colour, their shape, their light.

From that moment on,
Light-brown eyes became
My favourite eyes.

I was falling,
Unknowingly

I saw the way they stayed calm and steady
Whenever you talked to me about something serious,
I saw the way they widen and lighten,
Whenever you laughed,
I saw them, and I miss them.

I miss the way they used to talk to me, and
Tell me things,
Things about you,
Things I never told you about,
But wish I did.

Things I still think about telling you now,
But don't think I should or would,
Because they aren't mine anymore,

Still,

I wonder how they would make me feel now,
Would they still tell me things?
Things about your heart and soul,
Things they told me before and
I wasn't wrong about,
Things I admired you for,

How good of a father you would make
How good of a friend you must be
How good of a heart you have.

I saw you.
I saw the way you looked at children,
Whenever you held them in your arms,
I saw the way you loved them
Even though they weren't yours
I saw the way you laughed
In the pictures next to your friends
I saw you.

If only,
If only I knew
How much I liked you,

I would have acted on my impulses and
Confessed all my fears.

I would have confessed how much
I also wanted to kiss you that day
At the metro station,
I would have confessed, how happy
I was after receiving that text message,
I would have confessed all my truths.

How you never made me feel bored,
How happy and excited I would get,
Whenever you texted me, and
How all of that was new to me and
Scaring me.

I might not have seen my feelings
For what they were,
But I am sure I saw you,
Perhaps only
Unknowingly,

Still,
I am glad I laid eyes on you.

With truth, we can heal

Whatever it is you are holding from me,
Be truthful, for with truth, we can heal.

Don't put on a mask,
When I can still see, through your eyes.

Don't draw the line, when
I can still feel our hands, clasping
Under the sun on that backyard table,
Meeting for the first time, slightly,

Then,
We let go of the shame,
And held on for as long as we could.

We shared silly stories, and
Deepest truths,

We were alone, and
You were you,
You were vulnerable, on those rare occasions
And that is when I found you the more beautiful, for

I saw a loving man, and he
Made me feel at home,
I realised that underneath that carapace,
There is a huge man,
A man who can weep,

And for me, that is what makes him the strongest.

So, whatever it is you're holding from me,
Be truthful, for with truth we can heal.

My only protector

I am my protector,
My only protector.
My love is my comfort
My love is my home,
But I am my only protector.

He sees and cares for me,
He eases and soothes me,
He cures and softens me,
But I am my only protector.

I love his manner and armour
I love his power and sour,
I love the way he makes me feel, but
But I am my only protector.

The love of my imagination

The love of my imagination is beautiful and calm,
Is funny and wholly and
We hold for hours,
The love of my imagination;

We laugh and dance,
I do things, only he can make me do
We kiss and hug,
With tears and fears,
The love of my imagination;

He leaves and I go,
When he is back, I am all his
To love till the morning,
The love of my imagination;

I caress his head with tenderness,
I kiss his nose with gentleness,
Then,
I arrive on his lips and
There I stay,
I let go of all my fears and
We become a synchrony;
The love of my imagination
You are the only kind.

How to know

How to know, when to know
That is my question,
My only question
When what I have feels like love;

How to know, when to know when I feel
Bold but hold some creeping fears;

How to know, when to know when this power
Rushes through me and
I fear losing control;
When I want to stay true but
Desire to have it all;
When I want to know him slowly but
Want to lay on him too;

How to know, when to know,
When I am young and he is too;
When we feel so in tune but still argue.

How to know, when to know
That it is you my heart wants to choose.

How to know, when to know
That is my question, my only question.

What, am I

Am I broken?
For having seen him in you!
Am I broken for even saying these things?
For having fallen for you,
As I saw him in you?

Whatever am I,
I don't want you to be him,
Whatever am I,
I want you to understand what a woman is,
Because I want to fall, but
For someone who saw further than him.

I know this comes, without any warnings,
I know it might sound, like
I have some dad issues and
I might, but that doesn't define me,
That doesn't make me weak.

I have layers, I know,
I have fears, but
They aren't paranoia,
They are the products of my experience,
They are the products of my upbringing and
I am working on them,
I am owning them,
So that I can become a better one.

My heart is spilling the truths,
So don't find me a weird one,
I am just trying to heal my wounds,
I am just trying to find my routes,
And not wait for you
To uncover them for me,
They are mine to pursue.

I need to unpack and sort my issues,
I need to stay true and focus on my virtues,
I need to find the root of this power source
I know I hold, and
So, if at times, I feel like I am losing it,
I know that I have it,
I know that I am it;
Love above all else.

My mind and I

It doesn't stop,
It is in a race,
Perhaps I need some space,
But
What am I to do with all these rushing thoughts,
Crossing my mind at a high speed.

I might need some rest,
But
Before that
I got to pull this all out,
I gotta put it on the paper,
Because that is what I know,
And how I feel whole;
So, God let me heal;
Let me be here and reveal.

I love you, Dad.

I love you dad, but there are some
Tears that still aren't dry;
I love you dad, but
They are some things,
I still can't fully understand.

Know that I have forgiven you but
Forgetting is still an issue.

I am one of your nine children and
I know you didn't fight for us all the same,
Because we didn't all
Grow up under the same wing,
We didn't all grow up under your wing;
We were spread into this world,
Into five separate wombs and
This is one of the things I once
Struggled with but, now am in awe;

I feel that how we love you, also,
Isn't the same, because,
We didn't all receive it
The same;
Not in the same way,
Not with the same force,
Not under the same house.

Some had less, some saw you less, and
Some know you less;
Maybe I am putting too many words into this,
But they are the truths;
I know it,
We all, know it,
We just don't utter it.

I have seen you in your best and worst behaviour,
I have seen your rage and your love and
Sometimes wish – a lot of times wish -
They had also experienced this type of love;

But,
I can't change that,
In the same way, I can't change the fact that,
I was the only one who saw you on that chair.
Who had to hold back her tears and stand still.

I still remember all those nights,
We went into the woods, searching,
All those nights we were on the road, alone
All those nights we drove home,
Just to go back again
Those, again and again, were killing me, dad
They were ripping me,
They were ripping us,
I just didn't tell you,
I just *didn't know how to.*

I was afraid;
Afraid of your view,
Afraid of us arguing,
Afraid of losing you.

Nevertheless,
I know now, that that was wrong,
That what I needed was home
That what I needed was peace,
But I was too afraid to ask.
I was *too afraid to rise.*

I hope you remember those nights too,
I know you do, but
Now, I want us to heal and
for that to happen,
We both need to be real,
We both need to reveal.

I don't know if you have figured that out yet,
But I am here if one day you want to talk;
If one day you want to spill out your truths,
I will be here.

I know you thought that I was mature enough,
But Dad, I was in pain too.
I was suffering,
I was hurt,
I just didn't let you know, and that *was my mistake*

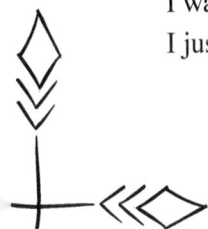

Perhaps, *in some way,* I, am, still, hurting, but
I want to do better too,
I want to use this pain for something anew.
Something I will be proud of,
Something I will leave behind for someone;
Someone like you,
Someone like me.

Someone who loved her dad,
But didn't know how to *impose limits,*
Someone who didn't claim her spirit,
Someone who sometimes,
Still struggles to tell him no, but
Knows better now and *does so.*

Someone, who
Nevertheless, still roots for him,
Because he once was my hero too,
Whom I looked up to,
My go-to.

I have in me many lessons,
I have in me lessons for a lifetime,
Lessons I picked from you,
Lessons you taught me
Through your wrongdoings,
Lessons I picked from myself,
Because I too, was in the wrong
For not having owned my truths.

Nevertheless,
As the years went on, *I found my way through,*
I started to write,
And believe it or not, Dad, it started with you,
It started with writing about my traumas,
It started with writing about my forthcoming, and
My desire to overcome.

I sometimes do it out of the blue and
It doesn't always end up being what I intended it to
But it is always about my truths,
And for that, I am proud.

Know that this pain is past due, *but*
A hill, still to climb, thus
Forgiving and forgetting
Don't seem to appease dad,
For sometimes you are hit by
A piece of music, by
Someone's story, or even deeper, by
A random face, and
The emotions dad,
They just kick in from all sides,
So, *forgiving and forgetting become a facade, one*

Hard to conceal,
Hard to put a veil on,
But for more important news,
I don't want to,
I want to be real,
I want to own my truths.

For,
This pain has taught me things,
It has shown me some truths,
It has made me anew.

So, what I owe in the end, are many thanks;
To God – first
To my friends and family – second
And to my dad, nevertheless.

My heart

I rarely feel like not eating,
But these days,
I have been all over the place,
In a state that I can't explain;
My feelings are indefinable,
My mind wants it all,
All at the same time.

I don't know what is
This that I feel,
But it's undeniable,
It feels untenable;
After so many tries;
After so many years,
Whatever it is - I still feel the rise.

A heart full but still craving!

The moon and the earth

Like the moon and the earth,
That is how I feel every time,
I pause upon your fences.

Like the moon and the earth,
That is how I feel, every time,
I remember your face, and
Decide to pay you a visit.

Like the moon and the earth,
That is how I feel, every time
I stop by,
Admiring from a distance.

Like the moon, who fell for the earth,
That is how I feel, most nights;
So close and so far,
So filled with longing,
So filled with love and life.

Like the moon and the earth,
That is how I feel, as
I take the last glance;
Done for the night, but
Missing you already.

Capricorn man

I love our we connected,
Instantly but deeply over time.

I love how we argued,
A virgo and a capricorn
Two earth signs, certain in
Their own way.

I love how with time,
You started to show me who you are,
You began to melt, and
Allowed me to write on
Your forehead,
Remember?

I love how I was the only one in the group,
You listened to, paid attention to and
Allowed to get to know you.

I loved all of that and stood by you,
Even though we argued half of the time.

I love how in a short time you
Began to make me laugh, and shout too;
They started to notice and criticised but
I paid them little attention, for

I knew the effect I could have on you,
Because I too, am an earth sign, and
Know my power.

I love that you didn't interrupt me, when
We stood at the front and
I left you with only two slides;
It wasn't my intention, but
Somehow you understood,
Without my explanation.

That is why, I feel that you are my equal,
Because you spotted all my faults and
All my glory;
And I was equally right.

Learning to love

Since young that I have had this feeling
Of wanting to please and prove
Of wanting to make him proud;
But this looking for approval
Has led me to places.

This wanting to please has robbed me of years,
Years of not knowing how to be,
Years of not owning my truths,
Years of not knowing who to be and how to say no,
But now, more than ever,

I need to figure this shit out, because
I feel the same way about you too;
Having you pleased,
Having your approval,
Having *your* love.

But the truth is,
I have to do these things for myself first,
Because I don't want to become that girl again,
The one who loved someone more than herself,
The one who lived afraid of her true self,

So, I say no more.

I want to learn how to love,
Without the feeling of
Wanting to please, of
Wanting to impress,
I don't need that stress,
I know what I possess.

So, I say no more.

I want to be sure that if you or someone,
Chooses to get to know me,
It's because they saw and see something in me;
Something they value and respect
Something I know I have and uplift.

I don't want to live in fear,
Afraid that may be,
We don't have many days left;
Afraid of you leaving.

I vow to work on myself,
To become a better me
For us, but for me first.

I am enough and
Don't want to feel any other way;
If, one day I do, I will find my way,
Because, I just am, enough;

It's time to
Value her, because
If I don't,
How can anyone?
How can you?

Now and always
I want to remember that this, *is*
And has been a long journey;
One I am still travelling,
One, we all should travel;
One that as a woman,
Feels indispensable.

Body and soul

What is this that I am feeling?
That makes my inside thighs tighten,
My body sink,
Calling for someone,
Someone I never had,
Someone who is too far.

What if,
It is just me who feels this way,
This pain and pleasure
That I can't explain,
This feeling that
I haven't met before,
This way of thinking,
I can't quite comprehend.

These, somehow persistent thoughts,
That I *can't put on a knot,*
This aching force,
That owns me for days.

How come;
How can *this feeling be so solemn,*
And abnormal too;
What have I got myself into?

Us

Before I said
What is love, without some thorny issues,
But let me rephrase it,
What I mean is –

I don't want easy;
I don't do easy; It just isn't me;
What I want, is worth.

What I want, is for us to know
That we can always lean on each other, and
That love, like everything else,
Comes with highs and lows, but

I am willing to do the work
And you need to,
Otherwise it won't work.

And if, we do work,
I promise that I will play it;
If one day we happen as I preview,
I will play it.

If one day, I place a hand on your left,
An ear over your chest, and
Listen to your heartbeat – I will play it.

If one day what is in my head plays out
I will stop time and sing it.

The search

It never stops, it hasn't stopped,
This searching, this looking for myself,
This missing thing,
I don't know what to call,
This incessant but important search.

At times, I feel like I know it,
Like I have it,
Like I know her now
And grasped who she is.

But then, those days come,
Where I am searching for her, again,
Interrogating myself,
Who are you,
What do you want, and
Why is this notion so important?

I search within,
I write about it,
I dive deep,
But she is a hard one to reach;
A hard one to get a hold of.

Her heart is full, but searches for more,
It is like something is missing,
Something she can't understand,
Something so thin and so big;
Something she can't demystify.

Whatever is it you are looking for,
I hope you find it and grab it;
I don't know if it's love, self-love,
Or any other variations of love,
Some days, it just feels empty,
And I look, I truly do, but
It is just empty, it runs away,

Like a tiny feather,
So sensitive, so light, that I can't catch;

Why do you run?
Why do you have to escape?
Why can't you stay forever?

Why do I have to search for you all the time,
Why are we so unsatisfied; *hard to define;*
Why? Is it just me?

Laid in bed

Laid in bed are two melanin bodies;
A chest rising,
His eyes staring up,
His face is unreadable,
His mind – processing, contemplating,
What they just vivid;

Down on his chest,
Rests a girl with curly hair;
She smiles but it is a small one,
In her head,
She is going through
What they just lived;

How magic that was;
How the way they cared for each other,
Just felt out of this world, and
How they have been about it, just
Feels like yesterday; certain they are in a dream.

Their chests, rising
Their minds, racing, recalling
Those interlocked eyes;
Those bonded bodies,
Meeting for the first time.

Two bodies intertwined

An air of silence,
In a place filled with tremendous feelings;
Some time passes then he asks –
You, okay?
She blinks, nods and muffles a –
Mmm;

That's all she can do;
And with that little sound
She conveyed to him,
All that she means;

But then,
Knowing how he is,
She turns her face up – *looking him in the eyes;*
They are happy, they are calm, *she sees;*

She reads him for a moment,
Then, lies back on his chest
Smiling in abundance;

Why do we need words for moments like this;
When we feel so whole,
When we expand with every little breath;

Soaked with joy,
When they lay so calm
In each other's arms,
Because finally came their time,
Finally, it's wintertime,
Their favourite season.

A persisting feeling

I never thought,
I wouldn't be over it by now
And admitting that,
Used to make me feel embarrassed
Because it has been more than seven years
But somehow you stayed inside my mind,
In all these years.

I never thought that seeing you again
Would create this mess inside of me;
I never thought that resisting something
Could make it so persistent.

From the bottom up

I see life as art;
I use it to create art,
because in art,
I find myself;

Through art,
I see myself;
I allow myself.

When I write, I release my pain;
I revive my sorrows;

I find hope and courage as
I go down those lines, and
I grab it, I grab it
But sometimes,
Life comes down with heavy loads,
That tries to scramble down my words
And take me down a hill,
Into a hole,
But I am strong, so
I pull the rope;

I hold it tight! and
From the bottom up
I make my way out,
I rise like the sun.

Find your art, find your way out, and
Rise like a star.

Life givers

I have some questions, questions I shouldn't have to ask;
I am looking for answers, answers I shouldn't have to search;
To why so many women are killed at the hands of a man?
To why some men are so cruel.

Don't find me embittered,
For what I am, is distinguishably hit,
For what I feel, is something deeper than rage,
That leaves me crying for days, non-stop.

I try to move on, but the same news keeps staring me in the face;
I try to control my rage, but *this seems* too unfair to forsake
For all they are, are women, no less than men,
For all they want, is the same respect.

Stop abusing us,
Stop using your physical strength against us,
We are not strangers,
We are life givers;
We birthed you all.

So, please show some respect;
Show some affection and
Don't take away our lives,
One of us gave you yours!
And, please make me understand,
How can their soul ever find peace?
How are we going to stop this?

Finding hope in times of pain

In my writings, I hope you find peace in times of pain,
I hope you come to understand that you are not alone;
That loss cuts us all,
Sometimes, in ways deeper than others,
Sometimes, in some places more than others.

We all have things we
Wish to bury, things
We have put a past over,
But it's there,
And when it surfaces,
It breaks through,
Like an unmissable glass,
It runs down your cheeks, like lava,
Uncontainable;

You try to hold it,
But the river has found its joint;
Its time has come,
And there is no other way but to let it run;

Let it run, for when you are done,
You will find a strength that
Was buried within your nature;

You will gain savageness.
You will learn that nothing is irrevocable,
Only death;

You will live not only for yourself,
But to honour those who aren't here anymore,
Because if they could,
They would make it damn worth,
I dare say.

Mom

Mom, I can't fully express
How much I want to have you near,
How much I want you, to also achieve your dreams.

I know you suffer; I know you are anxious,
I know your heart wants more,
I know that.

I know you would work hard,
Till you can't anymore,
But I don't know what to do,
Apart from asking God to make your dream come true,
And pray to him to give you patience.

It is hard, I know.
I can't begin to think it!
Because truly,
Only you know what it has actually
Been for you to support some things,
We have gone through…
Mom, stay strong and hang in there.
I will make your dream come true.

Now, that it's two of us

What did you put into me?
What is it about you,
That got me this way,

Is it your heart?
Because,
I swear I can feel it!
I swear I am in it
I swear I can hear it.

What are we going to do,
Now that it's two of us!
Loving you more than ever,
Is what I do, when I thought that,
That was even.

How far can one's love go?
I don't care.
I will let it stretch till it reaches mars,
Because with you, I met all of them,
In you, I found a beautiful place.

My grandma

My grandma,
Had a golden heart,
My grandma was a golden woman.

She had a tough life, but her heart,
Remained unchained,
For hurt can cause hurt,
And my grandma stayed alert.

She loved plainly,
Like an open art,
With a smile,
That could disarm harm;

She had so little,
She had nothing sometimes,
But her heart remained unchanged,
She didn't let poverty ruin
Her precious charm;

She had it all the time,
That duchenne smile,
That stretched across lines;

Oh, grandma, how we miss you!
How I miss you!

How I wish you were here,
And placed a kiss on my cheek;
A blessing on my head;
And a smile
For when I come by.

Love, blooms love

I have had some misfortune,
But they don't compare with the amount of love
I have collected
From all over the world,
From two continents
And three countries,
From my grandma to my mom and my aunt.

I can't compare love to anything;
Not even air suffices,
For life is more than a breath, and
Love compasses both.

I have seen what its absence can cause;
I have seen what its presence brings;
I have seen it in two separate houses;
One with a lot, one with little,
One with food for you to remain full for days,
But starving seemingly;

One with only water, sometimes,
But its people remained untainted and
Drunk from the well of love.

They possessed a kind of love that was simply it;
They walked around with it,
They just had it!

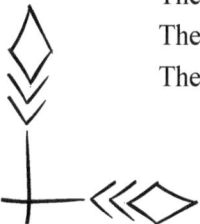

I don't know how it was planted,
But it remained like an oak;
That even on the days when
They had nothing but a simple dinner,
They shared laughter;
They laughed for not having.

Who does that? I, now ask, and you may too,
But they did, and I was there;
I was their guest,
I was their niece, and

I can tell you,
They never fought or argued
Over poverty;
They stayed as one,
Sewed in love;
United for a bigger cause
And I was being taught a lesson
I only now realise.

Things that money can't buy

Money can't buy you any virtues,
It doesn't stick for long, like love,
Whose roots can uproot any roof;

I saw love in my grandma's house,
I saw love in my grandma's eyes,
She loved me with little presents,
But big gestures.

She had very little when it comes to possessions,
But her gift was on another level,
Something many could benefit from,
For gifts like hers, last for
An entire life.

She has parted from this life,
But I still feel her arms;
I still remember her words, and
How happy she was every time,
I stopped by,
How happy I was every time,
She dropped by.

I was one of her precious possessions,
One of her many collections, and
Jumped and acted like a parrot,
Every time she entered our house.

I was little,
But lasting was the impression she was leaving on me,
Lasting is the love she poured into me,
And honour it I will, because *that* love
Made me a better person;
That love, made me more of a woman.

My grandma's house

What I, sometimes didn't have at my mom's house,
I found at my grandma's;

Back then, I didn't understand,
That this *thing* I was going there for
Was called love, affection,
Just what every child should have;

I was little but understood enough, that
There existed something, something
I needed,
Something that made me feel, indeed,

Something my mom, sometimes didn't have,
Because she was dealing with some
Deep shit,
And not everyone deals with pain like my grandma –
We are all built differently, and
She was my safe haven;

She had been where my mom was,
She had experimented,
What my mom was experimenting –
Men's infidelity;
Little was I and didn't
Understand my mom's pain
My mom's hurt, and
For my luck, my grandma was there,
To fill up the gap,
That another made;

My small but attentive mind
Was registering things,
That only now, I can put into sentences.

In the end

In the end, it all comes together,
In the end, it all makes sense,
When I remember how quiet
I would get whenever my grandpa
Recited us stories under the sky full of stars;

Now, it all makes sense,
My obsession with stories,
How in them, I found warmth;
Warmth of a life I was destined to live,
Because my ancestors themselves,
Couldn't put theirs onto paper;

They passed me a gift
I didn't know I had;
They shaped me,
Without my notice, but
My memory recalls it all,
And now it all makes sense.
Now, it all comes together.

A dancing crop

Alone, dances a maize
Unafraid of the wind,
It dances and swirls,
It dances, for me to notice;

Oh, wind!
Your breeze
Brings back memories,

My dry and yellow leaves, sense
Your wiggles, and they
Dance, unafraid;

Oh, wind!
Bless you, wind,
Bless this feeling,
For my ears need nothing but
This ease;

For my leaves crave nothing but
Your whizz,
To awaken their senses,
To remind them of their strength;

Oh, wind my husks know
Nothing, but lingering heat, and
Their silks are still alive, awaiting
On this thin, but strong stalk;

Oh, wind, oh, wind,
Come to me more often,
And take away my leaves
For I need both of this world
To stay alive,
Oh, wind.

A happy infancy

What a different but happy infancy,
What a beautiful but hard infancy,
That allows me to live a happy life,
That allows me to see, with different eyes
For I had nothing but old toys,
From my neighbours and others more;

What a different but human reality
What a different but continuous reality,
That many, like me, still live, away from the crowds,
Who hold nothing but brand-new toys,
Though, know little of happy infancy;

What a single but divided world
What a humble but rich infancy,
That taught me fields
I couldn't find in any books,
That has led me to places,
Filled with luxury,
Away from my crowds,
Whom, I will never forget.

Writing

A fulfilling but lonely task;
A discovery in the middle of
The night; that is writing,
Sometimes.
That is writing, oftentimes.

It heals, but
It also requires solitude that
Many won't understand;
Still, stay loyal to those fingers;

A stream of ideas,
On the land of the nile,
But drouth is also a fact;

An immense but secretive content
I once held away from the crowd, afraid of judgement;

Her smile

I heal with your smile,
Oh, girl,
Of golden eyes and curly hair;

In you, lies power
That like honey on trees,
You must dare to retrieve;

Oh, girl!
Of a sub-saharan descent
Your love is for some,
So, don't set out to find,
What you carry inside;

Oh, girl!
Of dark melanin
I pray that you sense,
What the future beholds,
For, I am seeing
Dazzling stars;

Oh, girl!
Of the desert land,
What miles have you travelled, and
What more is out there for you to conquer?

Kissing the sky

Up in the sky,
With the moon and the stars
That is where,
We used to find content
After a day of work
In the crop field;

At night,
Melody wasn't a problem
For cricket lords, lived
By our entrance;

Come to us oh, rain,
Come upon our fields and
Take away the sun; they sang.

Now, I know
They were a blessing
In disguise, those hot summer nights,
In my land,
Cape Verde.

Mother and child

Mother and child,
Those, whose infancies
Passed them by,
Those who learned how to mother
Before their time.

Mother and child,
Those, whose mothers
Were vaguely home,
For their bellies,
Needed the most;
For food was a priority.

Mother and child,
Whose pain
I know,
Whose days alone
At home,
Left them wondering of a land,
Where only happiness existed;

Where being a child, was the priority and
Their belly not so much of a burden,

Where childhood wasn't a task,
Mothering not their job, and
Loneliness, less of an occurrence.

Mother and child,
Your pain, I know
Your struggles,
Lay bare in memory,
And your strength is
My remedy,
On the days that I lack courage.

Mother and child,
Your reality,
Is still an occurrence,
For this world
Is but a fair place.

Symbols of brilliancy

We are also symbols of
Brilliancy,
People of colour,
Women, in general,
Queer and non-binary,
Immigrants,
All those who feel different.

The only hindrance is, perhaps, the place, the land, the
house, in which you were born;

We all can flourish in the right soil.

What a beautiful day

I went for a walk and found richness,
Of all sorts;
From the greenish of the leaves
To the colourful children,
Who played and honoured the sun.

I went for a walk and saw beautifulness,
In many forms,
On the ladies working out,
On their stamp and their stance
That denoted nothing
But confidence.

On the elders and their sunbathing routines,
That showed nothing but freedom,
On the mothers and their sons
As they played football unanimously.

I went for a walk.

My little brother

Tomorrow, you're turning eighteen;
What a date, my little brother;
Your birth was a blessing,
For mother was alone,
I, wasn't home and
Dad, not so close.

Your birth is a lesson,
For mother, became a different person,
More open-hearted and
I, more of a lion, when it comes
To my little sibling.

My little brother,
I would give you the world, but
Love is what I have, so
Hold in your heart,
My humble gift.

Freedom for both

When we live in a society
Where men, have been given
The power to lead for centuries,
Without any questioning, it leads
Many into thinking that
Women owe them
Some sort of obedience;

But, I sense danger in this
Sometimes, unconscious thinking,
That reigns many minds,
And governs many societies,
Stripping women of their freedom;

I seek freedom; I seek liberty, for both.

Some claim, it is their roles
As protectors;
But I say, protection shouldn't cost us our lives;
Protection shouldn't require compensation,
When it is done with pure intention.

If at any given point, you aid
A woman, don't ask for her phone number,
That should have been an act of humanity,
Not a service, so don't ask for anything in return;

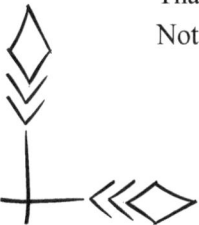

I am a woman, who feels hurt,
For I have seen too much disservice
Done to women, too many killings,
And many men still think this is us,
Playing victims, and that
Is what hurts more;

Your lack of understanding,
Your lack of action,
This never-ending silence;

So, I am begging,
Stand with us,
Stand with us because this
Is not just women's job;
It is on our shoulders,
But let's create a world
That is freer for both.

70

When things go sour

When you are young but have seen many things,
You start to drift off sometimes,
Questioning, if tomorrow
Will be a brighter day.

But I have faith, I have,
Nothing left if not faith;
That keeps me sane;
That allows me to breathe
And believe that, in time,
This dense smoke will
Perish, and
That life has led me here for a reason;
That this trajectory wasn't a
Coincidence.

I have realised that I must,
Collect my strength,
And not let bad occurrences
Offend my faith;
Take away my power and
My light to shine;

I have realised that
I am here not just to weep
When things go sour;
But to regenerate,
And be brave;
To embody the life I was given;
To honour the power I was entrusted.

A bigger cause

You lived, and
I survived
Those dense smokes
Invading our lungs, surrounding us;

Your heart stopped,
And I began to panic!
I leaned over, but you
Weren't responding,
So, I took unprecedented measures;

Hands shaking, I folded it
Into a fist and went over your heart,
Delivering hard,
Searching for your life,
Unaware of the heat and the flames.

That crushing sensation
Left me with no doubts
That love knows no logic, and
That I, could go even
Into a fire to bring you back;
To save your life
And we won in the end.

We won because,
It was a battle fought for love,
Supported by invisible forces,
So fear stood no chance.

We won because,
Our souls were one;
We won because love
Can tear down any obstacles,
And I finally understood.

You showed that you care

You joined me in the battle,
You joined me in the cause and
I couldn't ask for more,
I just needed to know
That you cared, so that I can love you,
Limitless.

You showed me that you care;
Now, I will show you, how far my love can go;
Now, I feel free;
Now, I can love you without any restraint,
Because that was the last thing I needed to know.

By God's hand

What a beautiful night, my love;
What a beautiful life we live.

We ought to stay grateful,
For we believed in our dreams;
We believed in our conviction,
That our paths didn't cross by accident;
That our love comes from above,
By a higher hand.

What a night full of stars;
The clouds have spared us the light,
The moon has presented us with her presence;
They have all given us the night,
So, let's celebrate,
Let's meet the milky way.

My mother's dream

I learned that my mother
Wanted to be a journalist;

Oh, but
What a trick world,
For that was my childhood
Dream, but unaware it
Was also hers;

I guess those umbilical cords
Tied up, not just our lives
But our dreams too;

And now,
Now, I understand why
You were so hard on us - *Jessica and me*
To prioritise school;

It wasn't just because you
Couldn't finish yours,
It was because you
Didn't want your daughters
To experience the regret you felt
Every time you watched TV;

A pain mixed with happiness
Because, afterwards
You had us instead;

An unconquered dream
That wasn't our fault,
But your parents
Low financial condition,
Mixed with a lack of
Ambition for schooled girls;

Mixed with a lack of perception that
A woman is more than just a housewife,
That a woman also holds in her
Intellectual power and
Not just a vagina;

But mom, stay calm,
For I intend to live
To my ultimate potential, for
I am making you a promise that
Your sacrifices weren't in vain;

That your battle to get us through school,
One by one,
When you had nothing but
Your hands to hold the hoe,
When you worked, hard
But your job didn't come
With a salary attached,
For you to see and
Cheer at the end of the month;

Mom, oh, Mom,
My brave Mom,

Know that
Your job wasn't less than any job,
It just didn't come with
A value attached to it,
According to our
World's norms;

But, nevertheless, it allowed you to raise
Your three children till
They became owners of their own life,
Till your girls became women and not
Just housewives;

What I've achieved,
Might be nothing for some,
But to read and to write is
For me beyond measure,
For since I was little
I sensed in me something
Strange, something to do
With unconquered dreams;

Thus,
For me to be able to conquer mine
Many had to put theirs aside,
Many had to labour day and night,
So that I could live up to mine;

So, mom
Never think
I don't valorise your sacrifices,
I know you don't,
But this is just a reminder.
Just a reminder mom.

The invisible power

The real power
Lies in going after
What you want,
With no guarantee
Of a happy tomorrow;

The disappointment
Turned into
Something different,
For courage
Succeeded expectation;

An unplanned happiness,
Found in following your innermost.

Higher

A hint, that together we
Can tackle anything;

A desire to wake up every day,
And live life;

Suddenly,
I am in a new world –
Smiling alone;
Smelling different flavours;

Reading the horizon and
Ready to embrace it
And put forth what
United us in the first place.

Stay as you are

Go as high as you can
But, please stay as you are,
For it's him, whom I love;

The genuine guy,
His distinct smile,
The singularity on his lips;

The beauty of his soul,
The way he sees life,
Combined with mine.

The journey

Lighter,
Unloading,
Aces,
I once
Held in secret;

Goddammit,
It feels so much better
To be in the open;
A worth seven years, spent
With tears and doubts,
Worth every penny;

A mystery gift, wrapped up with
A different fold;
A distinct view
That comes to all those willing
To pay the price.

For a better life

The *girl*
Who fears the red line;
Who runs from parts of her that
Resembles;
Who questions her decisions
For we can turn bad
When not held accountable;
Accustomed with
Being let off the hook.

Can one's essence become infested
Or curated for that matter?
Can forgiveness amend a man's heart?
Or is it the being who
Needs *first*
Repent of his sins,
Then search for the *exit*
That lives within;

I am the *son* who
Wants to end this
Vicious cycle,
Who wants to love
A woman at the time
So naturally
I must run from
The bloodline.

The lost sparrow

The sparrow who wants to rest,
But fears repetition for
She goes naturally
After those same nests and
Yet, fears resemblance.

One wants
To be better
Do better
But underneath
This work
Lies a dangerous
Mine,
Concealed with
The most
Rarest diamond
Rooted in mud.

Curving this
Tunnel,
Isn't easy
But slow I go,
Praying all along
Dight and night,
Searching for signs
Of the righteous pathway,
Aware of my back.

It's time

Bear with me
For now, is one a day;
Out of the shadow
She steps
Carrying out all that braveness
She once hid in the
Face of obedience;

Mind your head
For I am unbowing;
Brace yourself, thus
This is a new woman,
Less of a silence
You once so much praised;

Give me my rights!
No, no!
Get rid of that,
I am taking it!
Thus waiting
Has given me nothing
But years of bags
I still carry
Day in and day out,
Unloading one at a time.

Petals and castles

Pick up the pieces,
Lay them in circles and
Create a flower;
Pick up the petals
Hold them upright and
Build up a shelter;
Day in and day out
Till it becomes
A hell of a castle;

Cry out
The tears;
Cheer up
A little,
All in all
You have a great
Life;

Light up
That room,
Darkness
Only brings
Sad moods;

Enough with
Lamentations,
Life smiles
At those
Who get up
With intention.

Home

It's like you are unaware
Of the world around you
While all you need to understand it
Laid once before you,
But you didn't realise it,
Till something happens
And you return to it,
Only this time
Aware of the dictionary.

What are we not seeing?

They say, don't think about it too much;
But silence only increases death?
Why does mental health have to be a taboo?
Why do we ignore the Inner world?

Yes,
I am bothered by others' suffering
I am bothered by unspoken feelings
I am bothered by not seeing;
Our eyes don't lie, but we were never blinder;

You can't change the world; you worry too much!
Worry about you first - that is the message
Yes, I agree but doesn't everyone's story
Have a little of ourselves in it?

Perhaps it's why I care,
Perhaps it's why I try to stay
Aware, for I am not alone,
I need others to share, otherwise
The mind can become the enemy;

Now, we all wish you did,
Now, we all wish we saw,
Now, we are all here asking questions
That only you could give us the answers;

Among people, but still alone,
Among friends and family, but still unseen,
Between life and death;

That is, perhaps, how you felt;
In need of help, but not seeing it;
Just between you and yourself.
That is, perhaps, how you felt

What can we do to change?
What is left to hold?
How can *she* cope?
What is left to learn?

The things we don't say

Don't you feel alone? she asks;
I do, but sometimes,
It has to be this way...

What about you?
I do, but
I feel more alone
When I am surrounded by
People
And my soul misses someone;
That is when I feel alone.

Gathered or apart, you are never alone
You are in my heart; *whispers a voice*

But is that enough?
Isn't asking how you are more important!
For, how can I know?

Words, don't matter as action,
I am fond of words myself
But it's when I take action that
I feel brave;
It is when I share, that I am
Being human;

It's when he sees me
That I feel seen, and
In return, I do the same
To remind him of
The power, to stay aware
That we need each other;

Learn to love

Do you know what love means?
Do you really know what love means?
Do you truly know what love really means?

Then,
Let's switch places.
Now, tell me do you still love me?

...I don't want this love, my dear
Until you are able to feel my pain,
And see my pain,
Until then, I don't believe you truly love me;

Make up your mind!
It's me that you love, or the idea of me
Holding, never swerving
While you –
It pains me to say!

Don't proclaim your love;
It seems too fragile compared with mine
What I bear seems impossible for you to carry.
At least be bold and listen;

At least imagine us switching places;
Give me that honour,
Of seeing you suffering
A little bit, before you say that you
Love me;

I wonder,
Am I going crazy
For being this honest?
I am relinquishing to what you think,
Please learn to love.

Walking down the bush

Growing thick skin
Involves getting hurt,
Taking down paths, you were alert not to,
But felt curious enough to; then,

Without warning surges from the bushes
A golden sent serpent
Uncoiling like a beautiful monster
Coming your way;

Stunned, you can't run or move,
You yell for help
And about to get crushed
Or perhaps swallowed up
A hand grabs yours!
The same that warned you before.
How lucky you are.

The unbreakable bond

Awake I stomp,
Where is my sister, Mom -
Where is she?

My mom tries to hold me
But I'm uncontainable,
Out of control,
Looking in every corner,
Back and forth
Where is my sister,
Where is she?

My mom begins to talk,
She is here!
Where?
Here.

I breathe again
I begin to sustain;
You become a mother
When your little sister is born.

Some days

Nothing and all at the same time;
Lost between here and there,
No words seem to calm my mind;

This is when I wish I could read yours,
And perhaps find some contentment or courage
To master this rusty tongue
And ask for what I want;

My promises are all in vain
When I sense the slightest nuance;
I run fast and hold;
Betraying myself all again,
Unable to stay one and true,
In this clueless view;

The realisation

I love you!
This guttural sound
Came out of my mouth
But, it first, travelled through my back,

Vast my insides,
Erupting my entire organs,
But mainly
My ovaries!

A deep
And long string
Of infinite power
That comes from the most deepest
Well – Inner force.

That as women we go through life,
Most unaware;
But it's there and
When it kicks off,
It sits down
Like an unequal oak,
Large and robust.

The last letter

The last letter? – maybe, *but* truly

I want to say – I doubt it!
For, truly, you are the one
I want to share this journey with;

The one I want to share my
Thoughts with – fears and all;
The one I once loved but didn't know;
The one I still breathe deeply for;

From here on,
I don't know what lies ahead,
Perhaps, an end, perhaps, a start, *but*
I don't want it to end;

You changed my life;
For you, I cried, loads of times,
But I still feel those same things –
plus some more;

Sorry, for telling the world
But they will never know
Unless I have your consent;

Sometimes,
I feel like I am daydreaming,
Others, this feels like magic,
Something beyond passion;

I believe in the invisible and
At the same time, am afraid of being
Wrong, so I repeat –
I believe in the invisible;
I believe in the invisible;

Being honest.
Was what allowed *me* to exist
Being honest brought this to life
Being honest, unleashed my power
Being honest is the only thing I have
In this world filled with silence, so

I repeat, I believe in the invisible;
I believe *this* encounter wasn't a chance, even though
We don't know about tomorrow;
We already existed and
I already thanked God.

Love, by morning

My hair was messy
My face, wet, just washed
Some toothpaste, still on my chin, slightly;

He was about to go
But came up first, rushing,
we saw... and
I motioned, with
My index finger;

He smiled, understood what I meant,

Waiting on the bed I started kissing him when
They called me downstairs - really, now? I grunted
He smiled, knowing what it did to me;
...
Back again,
I just remembered feeling my pelvis melting down
A sensation no words can describe
A smile that tells me everything I need to know;

He does.
Looking at me as if I were the most sexiest woman on the
planet
With my black turban on the head,
Face just splashed with water,
No make-up on, just the truest me;

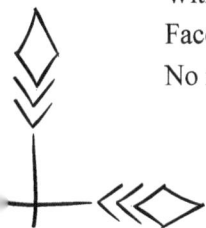

He is now gone and
I am thinking –
My stubborn heart was right.
My intuition was right.
My fearful mind was also right,
We are each other's best.

Why I feared.

See,
I found you in the middle of a hurricane,
You sensed some, but not all.
A pretty face and a hint of pain.
A beauty and also a beast,
The last one, you sensed well;

You came along and disrupted my norms,
My already messed-up world.
Don't be afraid... you said
I felt happy, tried not to, but
The mind was already charged.
Love hurts and you already have too much to
Deal with.

See,
You were my first,
And I, the product of a first
That...
I saw too many similarities, so
I decided to obey the mind.

I came and didn't tell you,
I thought about calling, when
I graduated, and lost my grandma
But I couldn't,
Fear, pride and hurt had already taken too much space,

I needed an exit;
I knew that no love could survive an
Invaded heart.

Sweet fruits are produced in
Fertile soils and I needed water.

See,
I needed watering,
But you stayed alive;
Inside a dry but resilient land.

As I started to nurture,
You began to be recalled more than ever;
Sweet and naughty dreams in the evening
Smile and happy thoughts as I worked, and
Memories drenching, everywhere I walk; Straight
I began to realise –
Someone is still a thing.

Then, happy but …
I began to think – *was I, also still a thing?*
Has what was once,
Cooled down
When I am still in flames?

See,
This is why
I lose my
Cool, whenever I try to explain;
I don't want to look like a fool
Who loved you in all these years,
But I dare anyway.

The way I love

Kiss me forever but
Hug me, far more
For I always knew, I would be happy
In those arms.

I don't want a super-man,
I want a man.
Easygoing but also hardworking
Chilled, when I am hotheaded and
Always able to calm me down.

When will I love him the most?
When he smiles like a child - sweet, real and beautiful.

When will I love him the most?
When he needs me the most;
I would just hug and kiss him
I would just hug and kiss him
Without words or talks.
Without words or talks.

Sisters in spirit

Those you come to know
As you rise and fall
Those you come upon with
Life's seasons;
Those *he* puts in your lane
To show you, how to love;

Those *he* blesses you with,
To allow you to see, *more* clearly
That life is love and love, the mean to everything.

Sisters in spirit, I have some.

The boy and the master

You were not put here, to satisfy.
But master, they are going to think that I am a …
You were not put here to satisfy.
But master, I don't want to look like…
You were not put here to satisfy.
But master, they will call me weak, less of a man, I…
You were not put here to satisfy.
Master! The boy looked down … you don't understand,
They are going to talk, and …
You were not put here to satisfy.
What if she calls me … the boy looked up.
You were not put here to satisfy.
I know master, but …

You have a life.
You have a feeling.
You have a duty.

If you betray your feelings
You betray yourself
If you obey your "friends" and betray your inner
You might not find your way back.

So, what do I do master?

Say, no.
Say, I have feelings for someone else.
I don't want to betray myself.
I have feelings for somebody else.

Okay, master.

And the boy walked away, full of courage, to be himself, regardless.

Women of tomorrow

Come on, get up and stand.
Let's show them that
We are going to be, do and ask for different;
That we are the fruits,
But of a stronger stalk

Let us be the lessons and the teachings
Let us plant with different seeds
Let us see that we have another father,
And that he wants us to yield,
And not let weeds tie-up
Our feet;

It's hard, I know,
But let's fall and
stand,
Let us get up stronger;
We know pain, it's not anew.

Come on, give me your hands.
Let's make a promise:
To be the women of tomorrow
The mothers of better sons
And greatest daughters,
The healers and the shielders
The fearless warriors,
The women of deserts.

Come, our ancestors are calling.
Let's give them what they want –
Women with a stronger sense of self.
Women of a better nation;

They are calling, can you hear?
It's time to pay attention
It's time for their tributes
What they carried we didn't,
What they supped we didn't and
What we know now is better,
It's freedom.
It's what they fought for
But couldn't savour, so
Let's stand up and howl
Let's do better.
Let's create some change with this rage.

Milton Keynes UK
Ingram Content Group UK Ltd.
UKHW020817260224
438492UK00015BA/710

9 781835 380079